# BY YOUR WORDS...

## PASTOR REGINA C. BRENT

By Your Words...

Copyright © May 2013; Revised February 2017
by Pastor Regina C. Brent

Published by Clay Bridges Press in Houston, TX.

All rights reserved. No part of this publication may be reproduced, stored in a retrieval system, or transmitted in any form by any means, electronic, mechanical, photocopy, recording, or otherwise, without the prior permission of the publisher, except as provided for by USA copyright law.

Scripture quotations are from the ESV® Bible (The Holy Bible, English Standard Version®), copyright © 2001 by Crossway, a publishing ministry of Good News Publishers. Used by permission. All rights reserved.

First Printing: 2017

ISBN 10: 1939815274
ISBN 13: 9781939815279
eISBN 10: 1939815282
eISBN 13: 9781939815286

Special Sales: Most Clay Bridges Press titles are available in special quantity discounts. Custom imprinting or excerpting can also be done to fit special needs. Contact Clay Bridges Press at info@lucidbooks.net.

## Dedication to the God Who is feared among the Nations

All darkness and tears just disappear
….By Your Words Lord By Your Words
The atmosphere is clean and clear
….By Your Words Lord By Your words
You are here and love is near
….By Your Words Lord By Your Words

Angelic hosts appear and all adhere
Humbly breathing in as heard
Quietly as they eagerly bow
Before Your Word

Nations at the sound awake
For all the earth to partake
In listening to God's Word around
The only heart where truth is found.

From God on His Holy mountain appear
And where all glory and love abound
Nations continue to rise and fall
But your word lives on to sound the call.

**-Pastor Regina C. Brent**

**One of my favorite verses in scripture can be found in Jeremiah 15:16.**

# Contents

Words .................................................................... 1

Heart Condition ..................................................... 5

The Arrogant and Prideful Heart ............................ 7

The Wise in Heart .................................................. 9

Instruction in Giving and Receiving the Prophetic Word .... 13

When to be Silent and When to Speak .................. 17

Leaders, Rulers, and Teachers ................................ 25

The Political Tongue ............................................. 27

A World of Words Inside the Airways ................... 33

The Provoking Tongue .......................................... 37

Anger and the Tongue ........................................... 41

The Destructive Tongue ........................................ 51

A Cursing Tongue for Hire ................................................ 57

Temptation and the Seducing Tongue ............................ 59

In Our Hearing .................................................................. 63

The Talkative Tongue ....................................................... 67

The Words of Others ........................................................ 69

Gossiping and Backbiting ................................................ 73

The Tongue that Ridicules ............................................... 77

The Tongue of Fools ......................................................... 81

Speaking Against God's Anointed ................................... 83

Riches ................................................................................. 85

The Unpardonable Sin Blaspheming the Holy Spirit ........... 87

Tongues of Frustration, Discouragement, and Discontent ... 91

Oaths and Vows ................................................................ 99

The Tongue of a Psalmist King David .......................... 103

Words in Song ................................................................ 105

The Word of God is Superior to Man .......................... 107

Prayer Our True Devotion ............................................ 109

The Promise and Command of God ............................ 113

Pastor Regina's Comments ............................................ 115

# WORDS

***Word given by the Lord on February 9, 2017***

"Come up higher above all the disorder and noise of confrontations and strife. I am here to give you peace in the midst of chaos and light in the midst of darkness. Find rest for your souls in My pasture; my field of dreams and visions. ***Come closer and listen to the words I speak above the people of the earth.*** Find faith in the heart of My word. Yesterday is past and tomorrow has hidden treasure---you will find My blessings there right in the glow of My promises."

Words are being spoken by human beings 24 hours a day, 7 days a week. Words pour out evidence of who we really are and what we are about; how we think and how we feel. There are words that ring true but are not true at all and words that are ignored or resented.

After reading "*By Your Words*", I pray that you will be able to take in God's truth and understand how important it is to know how to better communicate with God and man. Manners and etiquette should be taught as required reading and placed into practice in all schools and universities. ***Character plays a major role in good communication.***

Jesus said we will be held accountable for every word we speak whether good or evil. Good words are justified and condemning words return back upon the one who speaks it. A good tree produces good fruit and a bad tree bad fruit. **Matt. 12:33-37**. He compared different people as some who pour out good treasure and others who pour out evil treasure. Treasure is what everyone desires by choice and is held in the heart.

***God has a great concern about words that are being spoken of out of our mouths because He is a God of words and it is how He spoke creation into being.*** Communication between man to man either builds up or tear down relationships. Some of us are more accustomed to hearing what other voices have to say that we cannot hear what comes out of our own mouth; or, on the other hand, we are only interested in hearing our own voice and no one else's. We need to learn how to balance both; how to be good communicators and great listeners. It is more important that we speak what God has established in us through His word; for He is a God of balance and He always has the final word.

# Heart Condition

We must begin in the chamber from where our words originate; the heart. Words will ride upon the voice of an angel or the voice of the devil; sometimes both are spoken in the same mouth. It all depends upon the condition of the heart. This book will make your heart a heart of love not hate; blessing instead of cursing; a heart that builds up and not tear down; and instead of making war, release peace. What we eat physically and spiritually affects heart health. There are nutritionists to help us eat healthy food and God who feeds us spiritual food. Both are essential for our survival in this life.

# The Arrogant and Prideful Heart

The word of God in **Proverbs 19:21** speaks about man having many plans but the Lord God directs his steps and **Proverbs 3:5** tells us to trust the Lord *with our whole heart*, not leaning on our own understanding but acknowledging God in all that we say and do.

In **Genesis 11:1-8**, during the time of Noah, all of man spoke but one language. Their hearts were filled with pride and arrogance so they made plans together to build a tower reaching to heaven. Their motive was to make a name for themselves. They did not realize that it is impossible to try and climb up to God's level. He is sovereign. The word then said the Lord came down to observe this grand plan. He could see that man all spoke the same language; so if they were bold enough to scheme and devise such a plan for themselves at that moment, what would their ultimate plans be for the future? This is when God decided to confuse their language so that they would not understand one another. In other words, since they lacked understanding, why not all the more make it happen.

As a result, they were spread throughout the earth and cease from building. I see the Tower of Babel as a symbol of man's design that elevates them above God their Creator and whose heart is full of self where there is no longer room for God.

God's design and purpose is for His own creation and He will not give His glory to anyone. He wants us to seek His face. Our heart must reach for God in a humble state acknowledging His will and purpose as a grant Architect of divine design. This is a great example of how God hears our words and sees our actions. He moves according to His will bringing order and discipline holding us accountable. We are to make God's name great in the earth.

# The Wise in Heart

**Prov. 16:21-23**

In **Jeremiah 4:14** we see that wicked thoughts can abide in the heart. Listeners can be persuaded in two ways: (1) by lying lips or; (2) by the lips of wise men. God's wisdom gives insight to all who choose to receive His instruction and they will in turn capture the ears of the attentive increasing in equitable judgment and understanding. King Solomon is but one example. He only erred in judgment when he heard the word of the Lord but turned a deaf ear to idolatry.

An undisciplined child with poor manners and bad behavior was one of my mother's pet peeves. She would say, "This child has had no home training." Whenever we (my sisters and I) spoke out of turn, she use to say, "No comments from the peanut gallery." Do you remember this one? "I will wash your mouth out with soap!" **Prov. 16:23** says the heart gives out instructions to the mouth and give increase to our lips that we may be more convincing in motivating others. Lord let it be in a godly way. God's word can wash our mouths out and it will never leave a bad after taste. His word is like honey.

A wise heart speaks what is right. **Prov. 23:15-16.**

*God knows our thoughts and heart; nothing is hidden from Him. He examines the heart and knows what we will speak before we utter a word.* **Psalm 139:4.** *Just imagine God seeing your thoughts and saying, "Don't say it! Don't you dare speak it!"*

God knows our hidden secrets even when we are unfaithful to Him by turning away and abandoning Him to serve other gods. **Psm. 44:20-21.** If we are not faithful to Him and serve other gods, does He not know it? **2 Timothy 2:13** says even when we are not faithful to God; even then, His faithfulness still remains. He never opposes His own nature, will and character. We can take a lesson from Him. His friendship never fails.

God knows our heart better than we do. He is

a heart surgeon who searches the depths of man's heart. We only see what we want to see and tend to judge only by appearance. **I Sam. 16:7.** God knows our heart but do we seek to know His?

It is so easy for man to condemn others because some of us are all about appearance and believe certain prejudices. We pamper ourselves and pick out clothes and makeup to suit ourselves. All the pretty clothes and makeup will not hide who we really are when we open up our mouth. We often speak our own views about what we don't like about others or we are quick to judge others without really knowing who they are. God goes straight to the heart of the matter and instructs us to love our neighbors.

The human heart is connected to our thoughts and mouth. It is up to us to ask God for a pure heart like King David and learn how to bridle our tongue before we speak but first we would need a heart transplant. We must call on the heart surgeon, Jesus Christ.

***Wounded Hearts*** – Wounded hearts knows no bounds when expressing their pain and misery to others. Great sorrow brings on despair and comes out in words hurtful to others; it may be expressed through anger and rage, or sometimes without words at all, just sorrow. On the other hand, there are those who silently carry their words and wounds internally, isolate themselves; or like me, seek God for healing. Many people say they do not know how to pray. It is just pouring out your heart to God and allowing Him to do what He does best, restore your soul. Pray **Psalm 34:17-19**.

*Most people are more interested in their own issues rather than what God predestined them to do with the lives He has given to them.*

I truly believe that even though we may not admit it, we are sometimes guilty of our own troubles. We bring them on ourselves by what we say and do. God is more interested in giving us a word about how we can better ourselves to become more like Jesus Christ, grow with Him in a personal relationship, and love and support others in His great purpose and plans for us.

# Instruction in Giving and Receiving the Prophetic Word

When I was in the early stages of moving in the gifts of the spirit; most especially in prophecy, I use to repeat the prophecy to the same person over and over again every time I saw them until the Lord stopped me one day and said: "Tell them once and I will take it from there." Most times people will tell me that someone had already spoken that same word to them before. God will find another witness who will confirm His word. Repetitiveness is not necessary; be silent the next time and let the Lord take it from there. Jesus spoke about not using meaningless repetition in prayer as well. **Matthew 6:7**. If the person does not receive the word, shake the dust off your shoes and turn away. I had a friend once, she has now gone to be with the Lord. She gave a word from the Lord to someone and they rejected it. When she turned to walk away, the Spirit of God told her this was that person's last chance. The word of God warns us not to despise prophecy. **I Thes. 5:20**. Seek the Lord and pray about it in private.

God gives us a choice. We can either accept His word or reject it all together. In saying that, don't be offended or angry when the listener of the word does not accept God's counsel. You have done your part in presenting it to Him in love. **I Corin. 13:4-5** tells us what genuine love is as defined by God's word.

If you are slow of speech or have a problem with stuttering like Moses, God can use you. A friend of mine by the name of Frank Maurie died a few years ago. He stuttered but that didn't stop him from becoming and engineer and answering the call of God on his life to become a prophet. God doesn't care about perfect speech, He wants us to be obedient to His purpose and plan for our lives. He wants us to speak His truth and spread His word; but most of all, to live it out. Nothing stopped Frank from hearing the call of God on His life.

*Thoughts* - We take in and absorb a massive amount of words per day. We then pass words to one another with our tongue through gossip, lies, truth, news reports, social media, etc. Many times we parrot what people say without any knowledge of whether it be the truth or a lie. This is why we should study God's word, eat and digest it into our innermost being. The gift of discernment was one of the first gifts of the Spirit God gave to me.

**Thoughts have a filing cabinet that opens up the mouth and throws the file in someone's face just for the record.** We are all teachers of the tongue by what we say to others. People fall under the influence of the tongue sometimes by what we tell them or what they tell us. For this reason, we must guard what we say out of our mouth; especially around children.

# When to be Silent and When to Speak

God, in His infinite wisdom, helps us in His word. **Ecc. 3:7.**

*When to Speak –*

When prophesying: Speak when the Holy Spirit prompts you to speak (prophesying a word from the Lord). Procrastination is disobedience. I have heard testimonies of God telling some people to go back to the person a second time because they did not tell them what thus saith the Lord the first time.

Speak to God about the issues of your heart.

Speak life into situations and circumstances.

Boast in the words and deeds of the Lord Jesus Christ and not yourself.

Speak words that abide forever. From time to time we either forget what we say or what somebody else says to us but God's word is forever. From age to age man is still teaching, spreading, and delivering His message. **Isa. 40:6-8.**

Speak words of encouragement and edification.

Speak the truth in love.

Speak words of comfort by lifting up those who are bowed down and burdened and for those who mourn.

There are people who remain silent when they should speak up. If they have a problem or want to speak the truth about a matter, it is best that they divulge it and get it all out in the open. Say what is on your mind and resolve the matter quickly so that there are no misunderstandings in the future.

It was not until after my divorce that my ex-husband told me he had been angry for years about a matter involving something I did. If he had just spoken to me about it back then, we might have resolved the matter. Some people wait so long to open up their mouths, that when the person they had the problem with upon hearing about the matter days, weeks, months, and even years later cannot even remember what it was all about in the first place.

*When to be Silent –*

Be silent: When we keep repeating and replaying wounds and sins of ourselves and others in past years; sooner or later a deep root of bitterness will surface in the form of rage and it will be much harder to forgive and heal. Allow God to comfort and heal you through His word for His Spirit is called, "The Comforter."

**Proverbs 4:24** suggests we do not practice deceit with our mouth and not be dishonest or crafty.

We are not to make prideful boasts with our mouth but instead, allow others to see the Lord's goodness through what we say and do. **Prov. 27:2.**

We are not to be rude or easily angered.

*Listen to God's word in silence.*

Out of honor and respect for the Holy Spirit, be silent during praise and worship. [It is during those times that we must respect worshipers who are in tune with the Holy Spirit without any interruption]. In the 1980's, I was in worship when the Lord spoke to me about my ministry of deliverance.

Take advantage of your listening skills more than

concentrating on the words you want to speak.

When we assume facts not in evidence and are our hearts are filled with suspicions and error.

When someone else is speaking.

Silence can speak volumes in the world of our own imagination---which usually by the way runs away with us. One example is a doctor's diagnosis after an examination. The examination itself is stressful because you have not received the diagnosis yet. We always presume the worse scenario. I always pray off fear and anxiety and thank God for a good report before going to see a physician, dentist, or optometrist. Sometimes when our imagination runs away with us, our mouth soon follows along spouting out creative, fanciful, or unreasonable words and comments.

I would like to imagine this: If everyone in the world would be silent for one day, what would it be like? Impossible! It is not even on man's wish or bucket list. Maybe, just maybe, God could get a word in. The words of the Lord are pure. **Psalm 12:6**.

Jesus spoke to the Pharisees in **Matthew 12:33-34**. He called them a brood of vipers and made them realize that even though their hearts were filled with evil, they spoke good out of their mouths. God mirrors our hearts back to us. He has given to us, by His Spirit, the gift of discernment—His word of truth that finds our heart and flows deeply within our spirit and continues its way into the heart of others. Jesus called the Pharisees hypocrites because they honored Him with lip service and not truly from their hearts. **Matt. 15:8-9**. The Pharisees acted out of their own tradition and because of it, condemned Jesus' disciples in **Matthew 15:2**. Jesus told them to hear and understand. It is not what we eat physically or spiritually that defiles us but what comes out of our hearts that flows out of our mouths. Defile means to soil or dishonor and make unclean.

Sometimes what is genuinely in our hearts is not consistent with what comes out of our mouth. We should examine our own heart. Jesus explained further as Peter needed clarification. He said that everything going into the mouth is passed through the stomach and is eliminated. But the heart can pour out that which is unclean through the mouth. He then begins to list those things: evil thoughts, murder, adultery, fornication, theft, false witness, and slander. **Matt. 15:15-19**.

This reminds me of the old wives tales from the people in my hometown of Louisiana. They had sayings like, "If you drop silverware, it means company is coming." If your palm itches, you will receive money." Of course this is all nonsense but as a child and being quite immature, I believed them. Words are received as a teaching from the old ways of tradition handed down by our ancestors. Jesus was saying that the teachings of pure religion are one thing but what is more important is having a personal relationship with God that we may gain a better understanding of how to relate to Him and others. Jesus came to give understanding in the truth about what really makes people clean in the eyes of God. The Pharisees were too proud to admit they lacked understanding so they resented Jesus' teaching.

God's word is so powerful that His truth revealed is able to cleanse the sin in our heart, thoughts, and actions. The word washes. **Ephes. 5:25-26. Psalm 119:11** expresses the hidden treasure of God's word in our hearts which also washes and cleanses us from sin that we may not be tempted in any way.

Religious beliefs must reside in the fruit of God's Spirit: peace, patience, kindness, gentleness, love, joy, goodness, and self-control. This foundation sedates pride and arrogance in what we think we know and say.

The Pharisees were more concerned with the tradition of the elders than: 1) committing their lives and devotion to the will of God; 2) examining themselves rather than judging others; and 3) believing and living out their tradition rather than following Jesus' path and plan of salvation. People who don't seek to know God usually harden their hearts against Him. **Heb. 3:15**.

God proves His loves for us time and time again, He is not to be tested by His words or deeds. This is how we err in our heart, especially when we know what God requires of us. The people of Israel had received God's commands yet they hardened their hearts towards Him in the wilderness before Moses and one another. They continued to test God. **Exodus 17:7**.

We can either make war with our words or make peace and we err in our hearts when we have no knowledge of God's will or character. It should be our desire to seek it out.

# Leaders, Rulers, and Teachers

Some leaders of nations recently have come under the threat of the tongue from other nations. Spoken threats and the launching of missiles provoke other countries to war against one another and bring reprisals. A spark ignites and war is imminent. Some Muslims who are extremists said they would wipe Israel off the map and call America, "The Great Satan." Some nations accuse, scorn, and ridicule their leaders. The word of God says we are to submit to and pray for those who are in authority. **Romans 13:1-7** and **I Tim. 2:1-2**.

Over the centuries, nations, have boasted in their military might and power by threatening other nations with nuclear weapons. We have seen this demonstrated by President Kim Jong-Un of North Korea. Over the years, he has threatened war against the United States. Our response in word or deed could make the difference in deciding whether to have a peaceful resolution or impending war. Through prayer, God truly has the wisdom to abate this kind of volatile situation. Also, when rulers cause people to sin, they provoke God to anger. **I Kings 16:2.**

The Lord spoke to me a few months ago about pride in military power and how it is being demonstrated today---nations boasting in their strength and might. [i.e. the launching of missiles, soldiers marching in unison over global satellite and the tongues making threats to other nations]. He used the word 'Prowess". One ruler or king who boasts and threatens other nations gives rise to hatred and stirs up war. Other nations sometimes make counter measures and respond in kind; others seek to have peace talks. **Gal. 6:4.** God is our trust and He alone defends His people.

# The Political Tongue

We have seen the fallout from America's elections in 2017; especially the attitude of people whose candidate did not win. It is not a very pretty sight as harsh words of provocation and insult rang on and on from opposite sides of both parties in government. I pray that silent protests come back in style. The tone of our words says a lot about one's personality. It is almost like the expression, "tooting your own horn;" a symbol of self-exaltation or a trumpet or horn for the warning of war. Many politicians are adept in oral communication and skilled in motivational speeches. Political words should echo the voice of God as well as genuinely speak of the care, protection, and support for the people of the nation.

Today in this political environment, it is very unfortunate that people would rather believe the words of a politician than the word of God. Difference of opinions normally calls for a debate between two or more parties and will sometimes lead to arguments. I try to avoid opinions as much as possible. I don't believe in them, only the word of God and what He has to say. Christians are being attacked and persecuted for believing and spreading the gospel. Some people falsely believe that we are the ones who made up the gospel out of our own imagination. Jesus said that if they hated Him they would hate us also. I usually tell people who reject the word of God, "If you have a problem with God's word, go to God about it; He wrote the book." It is better that we suffer for obedience sake than for evil sake.

Unfortunately, we have experienced the 'war of the words' between political opponents both in accusation and criticism seesawing back and forth. Personal attacks and insulting remarks does not make a man or woman of integrity and only angers and frustrates the taxpayer who support government earnings in order to have a better more economical and protective way of life. The word of God says we must leave childish ways behind and move on to maturity.

The good news is that whatever God does in words and deeds, He always does it out of truth and unconditional love. He is our full assurance. Words fly into the atmosphere (cursing and blessing) and whatever takes flight must land somewhere; even birds know that. On the other hand, we find more good news in **Proverbs 26:2** which says that when there is no cause or reason behind the curse, it shall not come to pass. Jesus took all curses to the cross.

*Leaders and Rulers* are at best more accountable to the people who are in submission under them. **Proverbs 25:15.** The practice of self-control and gentleness subdues even the most obstinate resistance. A Ruler must not cause people to stumble or encourage and seduce people to sin against God. This is why the bible tells us to pray for our leaders.

I have often noticed on occasion that when leaders, presidents, and prime ministers are being questioned by the press, they are either vague or evasive when answering specific questions they do not want to address. Changing subjects usually gives them a way out as well.

We are all teachers of the tongue (rulers, parents,

teachers, pastors, co-workers, relatives, friends, etc. Each one influences us and passes words to our thoughts every single day. Our mind becomes full of information. We then pass words to one another with our tongue through lessons, gossip, lies, truth, comfort, etc. Many times we parrot what people say without any knowledge of whether it be the truth or a lie. This is why we should study the word of God, eat and digest it into our innermost being.

***Teachers***: When the honor is great, the responsibility is greater. Teachers are under an even stricter kind of judgment because they shape and mold minds through instruction. **James 3:1-2.**

The wrong interpretation of words can be settled by a simple question, "What do you mean by that?" Wrong interpretations of words sometimes raise up anger and eyebrows, rebuke, and frustration. Teachers are guilty of this sometimes. They tend to forget that their students are just students, not colleagues who can understand their intellectual rhetoric. Students who are shy will not say or ask anything and fall by the wayside in obtaining a decent grade. Other students relish in their own pride and arrogance in intellectual ability by showing off what they know making other students feel less astute. Students don't get to hire their own teachers and sometimes opposing beliefs and doctrines are inclined to collide. The next thing you know, there is a teacher/student debate thing going on in class. Just stay focused on the subject matter and asks God for understanding. Pray for all teachers.

I had a few teachers who had run-on sentenceitis (my own word). They spoke so fast I think I clocked some of them going about 80 miles per hour. I could not understand what they were saying.

Christian teachers and preachers will be held more accountable because what comes out of their mouths has great importance to God. We must handle the word of God accurately. It is so easy to sin in our speech and sinful words have such far reaching consequences. We cannot control our own tongue from speaking the issues of our heart but God's grace and wisdom from above can help us master untrustworthy, false, threatening, and evil words being spoken out of our mouths.

A great example of a God-fearing man can be found in the life of Ezra. Ezra was a priest and scribe descended from Aaron through Phinehas and Zadok. It is said of him in **Ezra 7:10** that he was a man whose heart's desire was to study the law of the Lord; and to not only study it but put it into practice. He taught God's statutes and ordinances in Israel. We must begin with a heart full of love, devotion and faithfulness to God.

# A World of Words Inside the Airways

The devil knows no bounds; he is sometimes called the Prince of the Air. He will infiltrate satellite dishes and world media if we are not careful of his strategies in our hearing. Read **Ephesians 2:2**. Talking machines call us day and night from collectors, telemarketers, or people wanting donations. They invade our privacy and we can't talk back.

*The Media*: Humans make a living at speaking words: Reporting Facts vs Opinion vs Fiction. For some news anchors and reporters all over the world, it may be difficult to separate the three without a full scale investigation. The audience would need a huge sifter to separate propaganda from the real deal. Reporters and journalists are all the more accountable because what they say influences the whole world whether it is the truth or a lie.

Machines carry thoughts from the heart through words inside TV's, radios, computers, etc. Sometimes we are able to overstate, magnify, stretch the truth, condemn, etc. Sometimes there are information and events that should be reported and are not reported and other times there are things that are reported which should be kept quiet i.e. classified information and intelligence from government. We are all guilty, including yours truly; but God finds a way of escape for us through His word. **Psalm 12:6**.

The media and individual journalists can also stir up people to take action on some issues. Their job is to inform but there are times when their tongues go too far: a) reporting classified and private information that should not be aired on a national or global scale; b) a tendency to slander individuals or businesses; c) be critical or unsympathetic on sensitive issues.

I thank God for news reports that inform us of what goes on in our own neighborhood as well as all over the world. I pray the news quite often for this nation and globally. We are able to weep and pray for those who experience disasters and loss and celebrate with those of whom God has blessed.

I never watch movies that are "R" rated. Profanity takes away from the whole subject matter and content making the story foul. Today the FCC places no restrictions on broadcasting profanity in the media. Years ago, they use to blot it out. I recently wrote them a letter admonishing this decision and told them how it would affect children and future generations. When children hear profanity, whether at home or in school and in the media; there is a 100% chance it will be a part of their own language with future generations to follow in their footsteps.

**Cyber Space**: Words spoken over cyber space has caused some to commit suicide. Videotaping someone in the privacy of their home or bullying someone on-line. It was through words on Facebook that protests in the Middle East got started. I had to counsel a mother whose daughter used profanity and mocked men on Facebook. God holds pastors accountable for correcting those under their charge. Facebook has been scrutinized for allowing people to publically post particular items. The tongue is like a runaway train that cannot be stopped and there is no such word as 'privacy' anymore.

This scripture is a lesson for servants and masters,

people in the workplace, or anyone who sit under the authority of others. **Eccles. 10:4**. Supervisors' tempers rise up against employees sometimes but scripture says we are to stand our position and keep our peace.

Many times we say too much and reveal secrets which hurt and wound others. We over-exaggerate and use words that are assumed to be true but are not true at all and when it is all said and done, many people end up being hurt in the end and the aftermath results in our words becoming unreliable and untrustworthy. **Prov. 13:3**.

**Matthew 4:4**: Man's appetite is not our only means of survival but every word spoken by God. The word of God is not just words but life to us all. Jesus said if we abide (live) in His word, we are His disciples.

# THE PROVOKING TONGUE

Provocation stirs up anger; disturbs and troubles the soul. This is a tongue likened to a cat-o-nine tail that lashes and whips out when someone least expects it. It steals peace and comfort from others and in most cases, is not satisfied until another tongue responds in kind. **Galatians 5:26** encourages us not to become so focused on ourselves that we provoke one another. A person who likes to provoke people is like a self-made champion who calls others to compete and join in with their rants and raves of anger and hatred or any other hidden dark issues of the heart. The only problem is that it only angers and torments the listeners who are not up to the challenge and only wants to live in peace without argument.

***The words of a Whisperer*:** If you really want to irritate or provoke someone, eye them while you are whispering to someone else. Even quiet unheard words can become loud and offensive; loud and insulting. Whispering provoke suspicion in some people.

***Remedy*:** Don't fan the flames by whispering. If you can't say anything without whispering, don't say it at all. **Prov. 18:8.**

*Provoking the Lord's Anger -*

**Deut. 4:25** tells us what provokes the Lord's anger: Making an idol in the form of anything. **Jer. 25:6.**

Do that which is evil in the sight of the Lord.

Satan does not like working alone, he wants partners and followers. It's no fun accusing and condemning yourself and others when you have no one else to share it with. It is like the old saying, "Misery loves company."

Both King David and Jesus' apostle Peter were trapped by Satan to speak what was not pleasing to God and it caused them to sin. In David's case, God gave him a choice of three judgments; with Peter, He confronted Satan head on.

Satan stood up against Israel and provoked David to number Israel. **I Chron. 21:2**. In doing so, God was displeased, so He struck Israel and spoke to Gad, David's seer. God had given David the choice of three of His judgments. Later on in the text, David repented in verses 16 and 17.

In **Matthew 16:21-23**, Peter rebuked the prophetic words that Jesus spoke out of his mouth. Jesus immediately knew who was speaking and told Satan he was an offense to Him for he did not set his mind in agreement with the will of God but with man's. Again in **Luke 22:31** Jesus foretold Peter's denial and said He would pray for him that his faith would not fail because Satan demanded permission to sift him like wheat.

We can either have the tongue of angels or tongue of the devil. Notice how God made a way of escape for King David and Peter. Even the chosen of God can make errors in our hearing and speaking; we must willingly accept God's judgment and correction. We must also know that Jesus is our Great Intercessor and He is always available to intervene on our behalf.

*Remedies*: Let us return to the Sermon on the Mount where Jesus spoke these words about the Gentle and the Peacemakers. **Matt. 5:5** and **Matt. 5:9**.

# Anger and the Tongue

I want to start with the most explosive emotion called 'anger.' It is a time bomb ticking that can go off at any time. It is so hard to hold back our tongue when someone or certain groups or situations provoke us to anger or; on the other hand, it may just stem from bad fruit on a family tree. Sometimes we end up in situations that are beyond our control (i.e. being laid off from work, the loss of a family member (especially murder), theft, etc.). **Prov. 19:19**.

Anger carries provocation, sorrow, resentment, revenge, hatred, etc. We see so much anger in the world today: a) People protesting against austerity measures set in place by their government; b) shootings in theaters, the workplace, and grade schools, etc. The biggest is fear of the unknown and speaking it out. Now we can really get in trouble with our mouths even before anything happens because there is destiny in the words we speak. Once something is said, you cannot take it back. Have you ever met someone who was so angry that no matter what you said, their anger only escalates? It's irrelevant to say, "I did not mean to say that" because words that are already spoken in haste with no thought behind it has already surfaced. **Prov. 12:18**.

Many times I will set a trap for my own tongue so that it won't run wild and uncontrollable. How? I try to think about what I am going to say before I say it and then respond. Sometimes, my mind will flow through God's word to find the solution. It is very beneficial to meditate upon God's word. The word of God is like honey on the lips and God makes wise the simple.

I have listed just a few examples of what makes some people angry:

When being corrected or disciplined. (Depends on the individual whether they will accept or reject it). God's kingdom is also the Department of Corrections. God is Father and parent. The tongue is hard to discipline but God desires that we not reject rebuke and correction as it is a sign of His love as our Father.

**Prov. 3:11-12. Prov. 19:18, 20.**

Invasion of privacy---theft (identity theft, home break-ins, etc.)

Road rage.

Religious beliefs that conflict with our own.

An irate supervisor or co-worker.

Spouse

Parent

Waiting in long lines.

Getting fired from your job.

Bill collectors.

Losing at sports and games; especially when unfairness and cheating is involved.

Not having your own way on everything; especially in relationships.

When someone lies to you.

Rush hour traffic and getting a traffic ticket.

When you find out that someone is talking out of turn about you or someone you love without prior knowledge.

A disagreeable person.

Mouths are where fists take aim. I love cowboy movies. Every time two or more cowboys have words with each other in anger; you ever notice that a fist immediately goes for the mouth or jaw. Anger hurts and mouths are containers not only for a war of words but for fists of fury that goes for broke; especially on teeth.

Anger and rage travels: One person may be angry at a particular individual but the fallout from this rage triggers another and travels to other individuals who had nothing at all to do with the matter. Anger, on occasion, will likely draw and direct a chorus of listeners. Have you ever had anyone jump down your throat for no reason? It is very unnerving. Anger, even in its dormant stage, runs hot like a volcano and spews out everywhere it flows.

The word of God says we are allowed to be angry (especially if it is righteous anger), just don't stay angry overnight because it opens the door to the devil. Sometimes we go into replay about an anger issue for years and bitterness takes root in the form of holding a grudge. We must stop talking about one incident for years on end. The word of God tells us not to let our anger cause us to commit sin. **Ephes. 4:26-27.**

My own remedy for anger is to go for long walks under God's sky allowing the wind to cool off my temper and knock some sense into me. It works.

Bible comparison: ***Cain and Abel*** –

An early incident of anger in the bible is found in **Genesis 4:3-7**. Sin and guilt brings on anger. In the case of Cain and Abel, Cain's anger towards God and a brother (worship in self-will). In the end Cain rose up and killed his brother. It was then that the first murder was committed in the bible. We can also envision this incident in a way of what we bring as an offering to our family members, our church family, to our government leaders, and to the Lord in this day and age. Will the offerings of our heart be filled with anger, bitterness, and unforgiveness or genuine love, mercy, and forgiveness? Abel brought a humble offering before the Lord while Cain, an offering full of pride and self-service. Cain could not see beyond his own selfish intent. He worked the field which is a symbol of a man of the earth. The issues of his heart desired the ground and what it would produce for him.

Cain heard the word of the Lord but his jealousy toward his brother's favor with God led him to become angry both towards God and his brother.

Cries for attention are a part of silent speech. Most people will not openly speak of it. God does not have favorites. If we just do what He says, we are all pleasing in His sight. The word of God says we don't have to kill anyone but one who hates his brother is a murderer nonetheless. **I John 3:15**.

As a result, God and Cain had words. There was a verbal communication between he and the Lord that led Cain to become very angry. I truly believe he was angry at himself. He knew he was in error. **Prov. 29:22**. The seriousness of this emotion of anger is found on the kingdom list of don'ts as the deeds of the flesh. **Galatians 5:19-21**.

Just like Cain, family members can harbor or hide resentment towards their own kin. Sooner or later it comes out of our mouth like a wave that has been lying dormant for years. Truth and lies collide into a war of the mind and comes out of the mouth into a war of words. It is very possible to both tell the truth and a lie out of the same mouth. Scripture also says out of the same mouth also comes blessings and curses. **James 3:10**.

Families can hear the word of the Lord but because of the noise of sin and shame, guilt, jealousy, or anger, they reject it. The battle from within is now exposed for all to see and hear. Family members want you to come around to their way of thinking and you want them to submit to God's way of thinking. God's word never fails or falls so although we may become discouraged about our testimony, seeds have been planted; we must wait for God to water them.

Even without saying the word hate or anger, actions and other words express its meaning very well. Believe me when I say, people know when you are angry. Someone could be talking to me over the telephone and I can pick up on anger. They are surprised when I mention it while we are speaking. It is also the same way with genuine love---actions and words say it all. You know without a doubt when someone loves you fully and completely. This I know because of my own relationship with God.

The person who holds rage is not only damaging himself emotionally but damaging others. Road rage is on the increase in this nation as well as rage against the government. A tongue that carries rage is destructive to others and especially to those who want to walk in peace. I had a Pastor who use to say, "Don't give people a piece of your mind; you need every part of it."

**Testimony**: My father died a few years ago. His

mouth was consistently full of rage, judgment, and anger. The rest of my family knew no peace when he was in the house. He use to turn the atmosphere into a battle field. He turned off decent programming on TV to the sport of Boxing; two men punching one another for other people's entertainment. This particular sport fed his anger and only added fuel to his rage. I still don't care for the sport today; especially since it is also called 'the fight.' People sometimes enhance their rage by watching violent movies or playing violent videos.

When emotions of the heart are rattled by a war of the words from someone filled with rage, a great distress occupies the atmosphere. I inherited my father's anger from my childhood well into adulthood. When I started studying the word of God and He filled me with His Spirit, one day He spoke to me and said, "Regina, get rid of the anger! It is putting sickness in your body." This was the day of my deliverance from anger. I try not to associate with people who have an anger issue because it is a snare for me. I just pray that God will deliver them.

We have heard it said that association brings on assimilation. This statement is so true. If you must be converted, give your life over to Jesus Christ and be transformed into His light and image. He is the Prince of Peace. Our own ways are in jeopardy when we associate with a man who is hot tempered. **Prov. 22:24-25.** Very few people can tolerate a hot head. Bad tempers carry destructive storms. Blessed is the man who is not easily provoked and whose heart holds the peace of God.

**Remedies**: We are to pray without anger or wrath in our hearts. **I Tim. 2:8.**

We are not to associate with people of corrupt character. **I Corin. 15:33.**

Harsh words shock the spirit and opens up conflict. The way I see harsh words is like a sudden tornado or a strong rush of a wave that overwhelms you when you least expect it. I have a strong personality so throughout my lifetime; God has blessed and surrounded me with very gentle, soft spoken people in order that I may have balance. **Prov. 15:1.**

*Reconciliation*: Jesus breaks the stronghold of hypocrisy when He spoke about presenting our offerings before Him. He said to first reconcile with our brother and make amends. We must remove all hatred, bitterness, and unforgiveness from our hearts before coming to His altar. **Matt. 5:23-24.**

Remember: It is because of anger that Moses did not enter the Promised Land.

# THE DESTRUCTIVE TONGUE

**James 3:7-8.**

*The Lying Tongue* –A lying tongue is like the poisonous tongue of an adder that cannot be controlled; except by the Spirit of God. Only the work of the Holy Spirit within us can bring this destructive force under control.

A liar, deceiver, and a mind filled with false information cannot stand in the midst of truth. Lies always fight its way back to another lie. There are no short-term liars unless one is willing to confess their sins and change their ways through repentance and genuine sorrow.

Fear and guilt from sin are the ammunition that fires the weapon of the tongue. Examples are: a) a spouse caught in adultery; b) a criminal with no regard for the consequences of his/her actions, etc. Lies are sometimes used as an excuse to escape bad behavior and when we don't want to face up to the truth about ourselves and/or others, we continue to live in the land of make-believe. Truth changes and transforms for the greater good and most people are either not ready for it or is in denial about it. Some people just don't care because self–interest holds dominion over everything and everyone else.

In **I Timothy 4:1-2**, the Spirit reveals that in the end times, many people will be deceived and fall away from godly instruction. They will pay heed to evil counsel and deception and will fall prey to liars and those who claim to be good but are inwardly wicked. The word of God says woe to those who call evil good and good evil. We see these in the media and in some governments. Lies make a wide path for corruption and deception to travel.

<u>Lies cost!</u> Lying destroys relationships and I, for one, don't want that brand on my lips. Lies, deception, and adultery cost me my marriage about 20 years ago. It can also cost you a living if you've been found lying on your resume. Once you are branded one, your life is not the same; in other words, lying may become habitual. It also carries a soiled reputation.

## The Destructive Tongue

After a time, people don't trust anything that comes out of your mouth anymore; it just goes in one ear and out the other. A lying mouth falsely covers up its true nature. God's truth is established on a firm foundation and lasts throughout all eternity but lies fall by the wayside and is soon forgotten. **Prov. 12:19.**

When people grow too accustomed to flattery, their lives are built upon candy canes and empty expectations. They rely so much upon flattery that when they no longer receive its complimentary misrepresentation of the facts, they are crushed. **Prov. 26:28.** All praise belongs to the Lord.

### *What the Lord hates -*

In **Prov. 12:22**, there are six things which the Lord hates but for the purposes of this book, I will list three: 1) a lying tongue; 2) a false witness and 3) one whose words gives rise to contention and dissension among brothers. **Prov. 6:16-19.**

"The perverted mouth" in **Proverbs 8:13**.

**Jer. 9:1-5**: Jeremiah wept and was angry (righteous anger) for the sins of his people. They continued in the bondage of sin and did not fear God. Lying, deceit, adultery, and idolatry had become a way of life. Jeremiah also had compassion. We lie when we have no knowledge of God and deception thwarts and resists the truth. We can actually teach our tongues to lie. **Jer. 9:5**.

### *Characteristics of a liar:*

When someone profess to love God but hates his brother. **I John 4:20**.

We have a choice of either serving God or serving the devil. The devil is void of truth and the father of lies. When we do not fear God, we are living a lie. **John 8:44**.

When we deceive ourselves by saying we are not a sinner. **I John 1:8** and **Romans 3:10-18**.

Over the years, we have heard about certain individuals and corporations who have obtained their wealth through deceptive means by swindling others out of their earnings (i.e. investments, employee's pensions, etc.). The ones who were caught either died or are in prison. **Prov. 21:6**. Invest in the truth of God's word and become rich in wisdom. The word of God says we are to be holy as God is holy. We are created in His image; and as His children, should model ourselves after Him. **Romans 3:10-18**.

Telling the truth is the devil's shame

## The Destructive Tongue

***Remedy***: **Ephes. 4:24-25.**

***Curse*** – defamation, misfortune, evil speech pronouncing doom, etc. An obscene word or words used in anger to offend someone. Curses are spoken to debase or dishonor people.

It is hard to find a godly man of integrity. If people are not lying to each other, they are lying to themselves and boasting about themselves. Many wear two masks of hypocrisy. Trust lies in the bosom and heart of God. Only He holds truth and the righteous way. If you have to believe in someone, believe in Him.

# A Cursing Tongue for Hire

**Numbers, Chapters 22, 23, and 24**

Great fear of Israel's numbers caused Moab to dread the sons of Israel. This is why God has not given us a spirit of fear. **2 Tim. 1:7**. Balak, the son of Zippor, was king of Moab at that time so he sent messengers to Balaam. Balak wanted Balaam to curse the people of Israel. This was a cursing tongue for hire. God set up 7 altars and met Balaam and he put a word in Balaam's mouth telling him to return to Balak. God turned the curse into a blessing on his tongue. We are all made in the image of God so when we curse others, we are cursing the image of God and His creation.

In judgments: Warnings against blaspheming

God and cursing humanity - **Exodus 22:28**.

I have heard a few Christians over the years use profanity and foul language through my experience in ministry. This topic must be addressed in the body of Christ. Many ministries and churches have lost members and money behind profanity and curses and I am one of them.

Profanity is like a boomerang that returns back to the tongue of its carrier. **Gen. 12:3**. Satan wants to speak through us just as God wants to speak through us. Choose your words wisely!

The apostle Peter cursed and swore in **Mark 14:66-72** when he denied he knew Jesus three (3) times. When we are in denial and refuse to hear the truth or accept it, our blood runs hot and we defend ourselves by lying. Even though we fail, God sees the good in our heart. He forgave Peter. He gave Peter keys to the kingdom that he would build His church. **Matt. 16:17-19**.

*Prayer* - **Psalm of David 12:1-5**.

# Temptation and the Seducing Tongue

Samson's moral weakness was for seductive women like Delilah. **Judges 16:4** says he loved a woman in the valley of Sorek, whose name was Delilah. The lords of the Philistines came to her with a plot against Samson. Two of the greatest motivators for most people: Lust and money. What a wonderful proposition made by tempting tongues. Deceit has the ability to use words pleasing to a heart full of lust and greed. Delilah was the bait for Samson and the Philistines were the hook to ensnare him. Each of them offered her eleven hundred shekels of silver. **Judges 16:5.** Now we know why Jesus said we cannot serve God and money. **Matt. 6:24.**

We all know the story of Samson and Delilah.

Day after day she wore him down with many attempts to find out where Samson's strength lies. She finally succeeded through her seducing words and persistence. Samson gave in and he told her the secret of his strength. **Judges 16:16-17**. The Philistines seized him, gouged out his eyes, brought him down to Gaza and bound him with bronze chains. He became a grinder in the prison.

God's gift to Samson was his strength. He was a Nazirite who could not cut his hair; for in it was the gift of strength by God to overthrow the Philistines. What God gives to us is for us and between God and each of us. Samson was safe as long as he did not reveal God's plans for His enemies.

This is what happens when we place the love of man above God and give in to lust and seduction. God gave Samson the secret of his power and strength; and even though he killed 1,000 Philistines with the jawbone of an ass, he could not overcome the seductive tongue of Delilah. Temptation was on both sides of the bed. Seductive tongues are very persuasive if you give into its charm. **Prov. 7:21-27**.

Seducers are people who lead others astray. A few examples are:

Evil spirits.

False teachers.

Sinful leaders who cause their followers to sin against God by seducing them away with false words and beliefs. The truth of God's word helps us to find a way of escape.

False prophets.

Wickedness is compared to a false mouth. **Prov. 6:12.**

*Pray* **Psalm 64:1-10.**

# In Our Hearing

We need to talk about hearing because what we and others say and hear affects our response either negatively or positively. Even in ministry, I find that students have a hard time comprehending what is being spoken from my teaching. I can look in someone's eyes and discern that they have no idea of what I was communicating so I would ask them whether or not they understood. Jesus experienced this also with His disciples. This is why teachers often ask, "Are there any questions?"

When I was in school, I use to get frustrated and think that I was slower or not as smart as the other students because I could not clearly understand what my teacher was saying about a certain topic in High School and was too embarrassed to raise my hand with a question for fear that others would think I was stupid. Some teachers have an innate ability to discern whether his/her instruction just went right over their heads.

The book of Job compares our ears to an examination tool for the words of others; similar to our tongue sampling and tasting food for flavor. **Job 12:11**.

Jesus and His disciples: **Spiritual Wisdom vs Earthly Teaching**

**Matthew 16:6-12**: Jesus warned His disciples to watch out and beware of the leaven (yeast) of the Pharisees and Sadducees. His disciples thought He was referring leavened bread. After Jesus explained (verses 11-12) that He did not speak to them concerning bread; they then understood that the leaven He was referring to was the teaching of the Pharisees and Sadducees.

*Mixed Messages*: A sentence, phrase or paragraph can be spoken but have different meanings to different people. Some people have a different mindset. Have you ever spoken to someone and they take your words out of context by twisting them into some negative message; or have you ever said anything and looked at a person's face and just knew they had no idea of what you were talking about? The message in their hearing gets mixed and confused and all of a sudden, they either get angry or they look at you as though you have just lost your mind. In those times, I have had to back off; start all over again (with a gentle voice mind you); and explain in a kind and teachable manner what I meant or intended to convey by the message communicated. Words taken out of context can frustrate, even anger those who are in communication with each other.

***Confusion***: If you don't know the answer to a question, especially when giving directions, **say so**. Don't pretend you know the answer and lead the person astray. Over the years, so many people have wasted my valuable time and money because they did not know the answer to my question. Instead of being honest and saying, "I don't know or I can't help you," they give erroneous information and I find myself lost and confused minutes later.

*Characteristics of people with darkened understanding*:

**Ephesians 4:17-18**: a) lacking in wisdom; b) people who separate themselves from God's counsel, His will and commands; and c) people who have hardened their hearts; d) people who are greedy; and

e) people who partake in every kind of immorality.

An ear that is not opened to discipline and a stubborn/hardened heart. **Prov. 5:12-13**.

**Remedy**: People who choose to hear reproof will not only live as wise men but will also live among them. **Prov. 15:31**.

# The Talkative Tongue

In our hearing, people sometimes shun talkative or for a more elaborate term, 'wordy' people because their time is valuable. I tell people all the time that my time is valuable. They tend to cut them off in the middle of a conversation; while others have the patience of Job and endure the lengthy oration. They are too kind to either walk away or say nothing at all.

OK, alright, I am getting to this. Pastors are guilty sometimes of having long sermons and people tend to fall asleep. I pray Lord this never happens to me. I guess that is why we yell so loud sometimes. I tell others that I don't need a microphone; God gifted me with an internal fog horn.

When I hear other pastors preach under the

anointing of the Holy Spirit, my attention is captured in the glory of God's word being spoken. I am moved in exhortation and joy, conviction and love. My soul contains the excitement for days on end, weeks, and even years. I will even repeat the words spoken because it had such a profound effect on me. The message is then spread to others by my own words. Of course, as a pastor I must say life application to God's will and His word is not only pleasing in serving Him but also in serving others.

**" *Try and stay awake!* "**

# The Words of Others

Over the years in ministry, people in the Body of Christ have tried to tell others what they should do, where they should be, or what church they should attend. I had a sister in Christ that told a couple who insisted she join the Children's Ministry that the Children's Ministry was not her call. The mature Christian already knows their destiny and is walking in the will of God. Listen carefully, just be prayerful. It is up to each individual to seek God for the answers; He holds the keys to our destiny in His kingdom. It is in your best interest and God's if we pray about it and let the Holy Spirit take the lead. We should pray for the gift of discernment **I Corin. 12:10** and especially for a discerning ear.

The High Priests were jealous because the apostles

were healing the sick and many miracles, signs and wonders occurred as people were added to the number of Believers. So they laid hands on the apostles and placed them in a public jail. Peter and the apostles were committed to preaching the gospel in obedience to God and their intentions were made clear to reject the words spoken to them by man to stop. Peter spoke this without fear of death. When he testified of their witness, they wanted to kill him but Gamaliel, a teacher of God's law and well respected by the people, intervened and reminded them that if indeed the will of God was being done through Peter and the apostles, no one should interfere or they would face consequences from the Lord. On the other hand, if they were acting out of human will, they would fail in their mission. I guess that placed the fear of God in them. God will always find a way of escape for His people.

Hearts that are filled with such devotion; so faithful and true, will never deny the first love of the Lord nor cease to speak and spread His word. He is the Lord of Hosts, the great I am. He will never deny us as long as we never deny Him. There was loyalty on both sides: Submission to God and His authority by Peter and the apostles and strict orders from man's authority in the case of the temple guard and the chief priests.

**Acts 5:12-38.**

When you read the bible or hear someone speak the word of God into your life, pray for understanding. **Colossians 1:9-12.** The Apostle Paul said "that before the Lord will give you understanding in everything." **2 Timothy 2:7.**

The expression, "to shoot your mouth off" is correct because the tongue is a weapon. The good news is that God has a heritage for the saints. He promises that no weapon shall prosper against us and every tongue that accuses or rise up against us will be condemned. **Isa. 54:17.**

***God's Care* in John 10:27-28**: As sheep in a Shepherd's pasture, we must be able to hear God's voice. We begin in His word. Jesus said His sheep listens to Him. He knows all those who are attentive and no harm shall befall them. We increase in faith by hearing God's word. **Romans 10:17.**

Jesus said in **Luke 6:27-28** to

Love those who hate us and oppose us.

Bless those who curse us.

Pray for those who willingly mistreat us.

The way in which we express our words can be either harmful or uplifting; be critical or given in grace by instruction and godly counsel; in anger instead of love. The Book of Ephesians tells us to give grace to the listener. **Ephes. 4:29**.

*My Prayer for the Brethren*: **Col. 3:15-16**. A truly grateful and thankful heart brings peace and joy. Let us use our mouths to fill the air and heaven with spiritual songs and hymns making music that is pleasing to the Lord.

# Gossiping and Backbiting

**Prov. 11:13.**

The tongue has power. **Prov. 18:21.** Words travel to and fro either building up or destroying reputations. Gossip starts with a spark and before you know it, becomes a raging fire. Gossip was just one of the Apostle Paul's burdens for the Corinthian Church. **2 Corin. 12: 20-21.**

Secrets are unprotected in the ears of a gossiper. They are guilty not only of exposing the most confidential information about anyone but intrude upon the privacy of others. Getting information is more important than giving it out for all to hear. They not only destroy people's reputations but suffer the loss of friends and associates in the process. In the end, everyone loses trust and respect for one another.

The backbiting tongue is compared to a north wind that brings forth rain and a tongue that brings forth an angry appearance. **Prov. 25:23**. A well-known modern day prophet said it even better. People degrade other people as a way of trying to resolve their own issues of low self-esteem. I had a sister in Christ that said it another way, "Someone wants to blow out your candle so theirs can shine brighter."

These tongues find ways of attacking the spirit, emotions, and reputations of others. Let us not become Absalom's at the gate who, through hypocrisy, rise up early to steal hearts away from people who truly want to have a healthy relationship with others, especially kings as in this case. **2 Samuel 15:1-6**. Absalom stood at the gate and turned the hearts of the people away from his father King David so he could take over his throne. Someone told David that Ahithophel and Absalom were among the conspirators. King David prayed that the Lord would cause Ahithophel's words or counsel to be insignificant and foolish. **2 Sam. 15:31**. Familiar spirits feed off of one another; it is how gossiping and backbiting gets started.

Gossip and backbiting is most prevalent in

small towns, corporations, small groups, churches, households and neighborhoods. Tongues that wage war against the brethren (family) have caused many ministries and churches to lose good people. It's destruction is felt from afar and has long term effects.

# The Tongue that Ridicules

In the Old Testament, the prophet Elijah was being ridiculed by young men coming out of the city. They mocked him by calling him bald head. **2 Kings 2:23-25**. The prophet cursed them in the name of the Lord. Just then, two female bears killed the lads. There is a scripture in proverbs about a curse that is without reason or cause; it shall not alight. In this one case, the curse had cause; the ridicule of God' chosen prophet.

Some people have nothing better to do in life but to downgrade others and poke fun at them. They are not only lacking in integrity, manners, and good taste but are also foolish and immature. If mockery were aimed in their direction, they would probably want to sue someone for defamation. Jesus spoke about treating others the way you would want to be treated in **Luke 6:31**. He also spoke about judging others in **Matthew 7:1-2**.

Some Jews were saying that Jesus was not a learned man nor had any education; but He had an answer that was not only truthful but divinely inspired and He made His position clear. We have a lot to learn from Jesus. **John 7:15-18**.

*The Apostle John's declaration*: **John 3:31-36**.

Unfortunately, young people in schools today are being bullied and talked about online. Some have committed suicide from this destructive tongue of technology. Do them a great service and give this book to them as an encouragement from the Lord. God says they are valuable and He has a deep abiding love for them. This is their true identity in Christ Jesus.

A clean tongue brings light and life into the earth so that when the mouth speaks the whole atmosphere changes to reflect the glory of God. This is how we release a wholesome holy communication to others; speaking God's voice.

Tackling the tongue is not hard when your heart-thoughts are activated and motivated by the Word of God. When someone has a question, you will be ready with an answer; the right answers. It helps you to make progress through the process.

The Word of God. **Heb. 4:12.** God wants to speak to us and through us by placing His word in our heart, thoughts, and mouth. God makes a way of escape for us through His life-giving word, the source of light and salvation. ***Prophesy divine words into your situations and into the earth!***

Pray **Psalm 19:14.**

Prophesy –

**Psalm 49:3.**

**Prov. 8:6-8.**

**Psalm 39:1.**

# The Tongue of Fools

**Eccles. 10:12-13.**
Fools write their own rule book that no normal person understands except other fools. **Prov. 10:21.** They lack wisdom and understanding and the desire of ever gaining any. Their heads are clouded over with false perceptions. Sound instruction is beyond their comprehension. They worship self and neglect the needy. They walk in error and wickedness. Corruption follows their path and their words are reprehensible. **Psalm 14:1** and **Isa. 32:6.**

The fool's heart refuses to accept God as their Creator. **Psalm 14:1.**

They speak nonsense and their hearts hold darkness.

They have no compassion for others. **Isaiah 32:6.**

# Speaking Against God's Anointed

The Lord hears every word others speak against His chosen people. See **Numbers, Chapter 12**. Miriam and Aaron spoke against Moses because he married a Cushite. The Lord then called out Miriam, Aaron, and Moses to speak to them. He told them that He speaks to his prophet Moses face to face and very clearly. Why were they not afraid to speak against His servant Moses? Leadership carries a great responsibility in itself and when the people on your staff or others question the leadership God has given to you, God intervenes. We must be careful in our verbal attacks against God's choice of leadership and not doubt who He has chosen. God's will can never be replaced, debated, or challenged.

The Lord's anger burned and when the cloud lifted, Miriam's skin was leprous; but Moses cried out for her healing after Aaron petitioned Moses not to hold the sin against them. Aaron admitted that they were foolish. Miriam was placed outside the camp for 7 days and restored back. **Matthew 7:1**.

God showed me in dreams and visions those in my ministry who were working against me many years ago. There were also a few times in my life when the Lord actually let me hear what people said about me in dreams but I never said anything to them, I just prayed. Depending on what they said about me, I either prayed for my own protection or prayed for their salvation. There were many times I prayed for myself in the event I was the one who erred instead. I like to cover all my bases. Read **Matt. 5:11-12**.

# RICHES

We are foolish to think that we will live forever. We must live each day as our last for the Word of God says that today is the day of salvation. Jesus told the _Parable of the Rich Fool_ in **Luke 12:16-20**. The rich man was so focused on his riches and where he should store them up; he decided to build larger barns to store his goods. He then declared to his soul by boasting that he had much for many years to come and that he should just relax and take his ease and enjoy it. Then the Lord stepped in and called him foolish for that very night his soul would be taken and no one would be able own what he had gathered. Someone said to me once years and years ago, "Nothing in this world is better than money." I responded, "Yes there is….good health."

A fool is his/her own worst enemy. Their mouths cause conflict and are full of fury. They are combative and ensnare those who are in the midst of them. **Prov. 18:6-7**. The lesson of this parable is found in verse 21. Our definition of treasure and Jesus's definition are two different things. We must be rich toward God.

You won't find too many people who will admit to being a liar or a fool or too many people brave or bold enough to tell them about their sinful way of life. Jesus said we should never call anyone a fool in **Matthew 5:22**. The word of God instructs us about the ways in which we can discern foolish words and actions. **Prov. 10:21**.

*Remedy*: If we gain understanding in what the will of God is, we are well on our way to recovery. **Ephes. 5:17**. The word of God says to keep from being foolish, we need to understand what the will of the Lord is as well as have a knowledge of who God is. **Prov. 8:5**. Pray for the gift of discernment and find wisdom in the Word of God.

# THE UNPARDONABLE SIN BLASPHEMING THE HOLY SPIRIT

**Matthew 12:24-32.**

For many years as a Christian, I did not know or understand what the sin of blaspheming the Holy Spirit was. I should have opened my mouth and asked. This should have been a time to speak. I never had any teaching or instruction on it.

*Blasphemy* is profaning the name of the Lord. It is evil or slanderous words and behavior towards anything holy and held sacred.

In the gospel of Jesus Christ, the Pharisees made a statement; they said about Jesus after He healed a demon-possessed man that He was the ruler of demons. Jesus explained to them that demons are not divided against themselves. He then told them that sin and blasphemy will be forgiven but one who speaks against the Spirit of God shall not be forgiven. **Matt. 12:31-32**.

**Testimony**: My own mother-in-law years back said out of her mouth that speaking in tongues were of the devil. This is blasphemy as speaking in tongues is one of the gifts of the Holy Spirit. **I Corin. 12:7-10**.

**Testimony**: There was a man who died of a massive heart attack alone in his home years back. He used to have a prominent position with a large oil and gas firm. He had a very deep threatening voice and a very intimidating personality. He hated the sight of me and kept passing a false rumor to department heads that I was a troublemaker. I just ignored him and tried to do the best job possible and prayed that my work ethic would override this false perception of me.

One day I entered the elevator and he was the only one inside. He said to me, after my department was undergoing a transition which included layoffs at the time, "What are you going to do about it?" I said, "I am going to pray." He then replied, "That won't do you any good." I never responded, only remained quiet. The Holy Spirit told me that he had just blasphemed Him. Instead of being angry, I felt sorry for him because I did not think he realized what he had just spoken out of his mouth. Jesus commands us to pray.

The tongue can become lethal when we don't know what the will of God is and what He does and does not desire for us to speak. The Word of God (obedience to that word) and prayer are the most basic and fundamental foundation of our Christian walk of faith. (Pray more for the fruit of self-control).

Because of this man's unbelief coming from his mouth, his statement caused him to:

Be a stumbling block to me in prayer. **Matthew 18:5-6.**

Nullify and invalidate the work of the Holy Spirit in hearing or answering my prayer and obeying the command of God to pray. **Luke 19:46; Mark 11:24.**

The apostle Paul's words in **I Thes. 5:16-18** shows us the more excellent way to use our words.

# Tongues of Frustration, Discouragement, and Discontent

There are three companions that will cause our faith to erode as well as spread to other tongues like a plague: They are (1) Frustration; (2) Discouragement; and (3) Discontent. Complaints not only find a home in these three but also promote building up more tongues who want to join in the chorus in following its direction.

### Frustration

Frustration brings on fatigue; you have to take a deep breath sometimes. It also diminishes faith. When we express our frustration with our tongue, it poses an even deeper burden on ourselves and others. Spoken words of frustration frustrate others. I associate this personality trait as one who is impatient and under a lot of stress. Here are some examples of items that I get frustrated and discouraged about.

Long lines in the check-out counter in a grocery store, the Dept. of Public Safety (driver's license), or department store. People with huge baskets of groceries in the 15 items or less aisle.

Looking for a new job.

When furniture and toys come unassembled and you have to not only figure out how to put it together but find instructions in English to assemble it.

Failing an important test.

Waiting for over an hour in the doctor's office after your appointment.

Telemarketers calling at all hours.

When traffic and public transportation makes you late for work or for an important interview.

When I am hungry and a restaurant brings me the wrong order or when the food and service was not to my liking.

Cannot get out of debt. It is sometimes of our own making unless some necessity in life comes up without our knowledge (i.e. TV goes out, need a new car, medical appointments, prescriptions, home repairs, etc.). After my lay off in the year 2000, I found out that there were a lot of things I could live without. We must distinguish our needs from our wants.

Time to stop putting off cleaning the house, washing the dishes, and washing clothes [old routines day after day].

When machines don't work properly [computers, washers and dryers, ATMs, vending machines, etc.].

When I cannot find where I placed a personal item I need in the house. (i.e. jewelry, shoes, clothing items, money, etc.).

*Third Party Interference*: Nothing frustrates people more than a third party interruption into a two party conversation; especially when a personal opinion is clearly unwarranted. Wait for an invitation or say nothing at all. It is the same way with suggestions. I often wondered if anyone ever read suggestions in a suggestion box or if it is just there to shut people up about their complaints. When I was just a kid in knee pants, whenever people gave silly suggestions that no one cared about, we use to say, "Place your suggestions in the 'suggestion box'." Now that I ponder on it, this statement is quite rude but not as crude as "If I wanted your suggestion, I would have asked for it." Common courtesy should be a required subject on all high school and college campuses. Pray that they be clothed in courtesy and refinement.

### *Discouragement*

Tongues that dash one's hopes and destroys one's self-confidence. Discouragement defined means to deprive of courage, hope, or confidence. The spirit of discouragement hinders our progress from ever coming out of bondage (sin, addictions, etc.). It also hinders our trust in God. I am getting discouraged just hearing about it. It erodes or eats up faith and prompts the tongue to speak negative words about ourselves and others. It can take root and spread spirits of depression, oppression, and heaviness.

Sometimes we discourage ourselves by saying negative words about ourselves. On the other hand, we become even more discouraged when people kick us when we are down or as they say, "Pour salt in the wound." Words that crush the spirit of man lowers our self-esteem, robs us of our faith, and place doubt and confusion in the mind of the hearer. It is a tongue that cuts faith and hope into pieces. Many people shy away from negative words, get angry, or just separate themselves from these words of woe. Some tongues are teachable and some are not. I pray that this write up is helping you because it sure is helping me.

Remember "Job's Comforters?" Job's response and concern to himself and his miserable comforters after he lost his home, family, and health was how much more time he would have to endure their torment by crushing him with their words. **Job 19:2.** Be careful of associations and dark counsel.

When we open our mouth, we must judge righteously. God is the Righteous Judge and our justice comes from His will and instruction. We must speak words in defense of those who are less fortunate, the sick and the needy. **Prov. 31:9.**

**Remedy**: Fear and anxiety is like an anchor in the heart but when we or someone else speaks a good and encouraging word, the heart is light and gay. **Prov. 12:25.**

### *Discontent*

### **Phil. 2:14**

Discontent is a restless craving for what one does not have or believe they have a right to have. People often find fault with themselves and others. We find fault with government and government leaders. The people of Israel grumbled against Moses and God **Exodus 16:6-7**; the scribes grumbled against Jesus and His apostles **Luke 5:30**. Discontent sets the tongue in a position to spread uncomplimentary and insulting words against others; even against the very people who are trying to help and protect them. We see this spirit operating in our world today. A lot of good it did to the people of Israel; it caused them to remain in the wilderness for 40 years and it was no picnic for Moses either.

Grumbling and complaining do not in any way solve problems. When employees grumble and complain, employers are angered at their discontent. Some will discredit your performance in an evaluation or fire you as troublemakers. God is angered by these spirits because it is a sign of unbelief that needs to be admonished and disciplined. With God, all things are possible. We must believe His word regardless of our trials and adversities. All the grumbling and complaining in the world will not solve problems, it only adds to an already very troubling atmosphere of disagreements. Nations have found that peace negotiations are preferred. I recommend fervent prayer.

## Tongues of Frustration, Discouragement, and Discontent

Contentment is a process we learn over the years through prayer and the Word of God. Patience and endurance brings us closer to contentment. The people of Israel were professional grumblers and complainers. God hears our grumbling. **Exodus 16:9-12** and **Numbers 17:5**. If we continue to live a life of discontent, we will overlook or fail to observe the good in ourselves and in others; we will be lacking in gratitude for what we do have; i.e. the goodness of the Lord and His grace, the beauty in God's grand design in creation. Personally, I would like some joy and laughter in my life. I have seen enough pain, anger, scorn, and suffering in my lifetime; especially from the media. I pray that the media would find stories that lift up the soul and bring joy and encouragement in our lives as people of the earth. There must be some balance between good news and bad news.

*Remedy from the Apostle Paul:* **Phil. 4:11-13**.

# OATHS AND VOWS

**Eccles. 5:4-5**

Some people who take oaths and vows are: Physicians, Presidents, Peace Officers, Boy Scouts and Girl Scouts, people enlisting into the military, etc. Another example is marriage vows. This is why God hates divorce. **Malachi 2:16.** God established the marriage covenant; He is a covenant God. **Matthew 5:33-37.** People are very discouraged and disappointed when others break their promises; God even more so because He is a faithful God of truth and promises.

THIS MUST BE OUR FERVENT DESIRE: **Proper Employment of the Tongue**

In **Proverbs 16:4**, pleasant words are compared

to a honeycomb, agreeable and kind to the soul and strong and sound to the bones. Character and integrity matters to God: If we are to abide in His dwelling place and on His holy mountain (His presence and in our hearts), **Psalm 15:1-5** says we are to –

Walk in integrity.

Speak the truth from our heart and not slander with our tongue.

Keep an oath.

Honor your neighbor.

Honor those who fear God.

If we genuinely want to honor God, let our mouth be thankful and call upon His name. Let our mouth make known His mighty deeds to the people of the earth and sing His praises. Let grateful hearts rejoice in the Lord. **Psalm 126:1-3**.

Instead of cursing, speak blessing and let all of God's creation who has breath praise His holy name.

### *Our confession* –Phil. 2:9-11

*Jesus declares* that everyone who confesses Him before men, He will confess them before His Father in heaven. Likewise, whoever denies Him before men, He will deny them before His Father who is in heaven. **Matthew 10:32-33**. For His word is always near to us in our mouths and hearts and that if we confess Jesus as our Lord and Savior while believing in our hearts that He was raised from the dead, we shall be saved. **Romans 10:8-10** goes on to say that the heart is a vessel that believes resulting in righteousness and with our mouth we confess, resulting in salvation. Every beat of our heart brings life to our body and soul. The heart is where life begins and ends. Let us fill it with our confession of faith.

# THE TONGUE OF A PSALMIST KING DAVID

All of David's psalms were heart cries to the Lord that only He and the Lord understood. This is what resembles a true and loyal relationship through communication. I prayed his psalms often in my lifetime. David attracted a considerable following of those who were in debt and discontented. **I Samuel 22:2**. God may be sending people your way that He may use you to make His path clear. How will you receive them?

David had the ability to lead and motivate others. He had a heart of worship, intercession, and repentance before God and when God favors you, people are drawn to your spirit. It takes great leadership to build an army out of such men. These men produced several more "mighty men." David's heart of worship and adoration gave him a tongue of praise to God. When he sinned, he did not deny it but went before God with a repentant heart. This adoration as a psalmist poured out as God's hand of deliverance was upon him when he sang for King Saul with his harp. His music and worship drove away the evil spirits from King Saul.

***For Edification and Exhortation***: David encouraged himself in the Lord when no one else would. He encouraged people who were downtrodden and hopeless; even though he was a fugitive from King Saul and on the run himself. He opened up his heart to be a friend to Jonathan, King Saul's son, and listened to the words of the prophet given to him by God. No matter that he was king of Israel, he humbled himself before God's word and listened. God loves humility and listeners. In spite of all of his battles and disappointments, his success was grounded in his ability to worship the Lord out of his heart. This worship was expressed in many of his psalms.

# Words in Song

Musical instruments have been complimenting and accentuating words and feelings for many musicians over the past centuries. We speak words, we write words down on paper, and we sing words—words in songs of sorrow and words in songs of celebration. Words that inspire songwriters to write more songs—words that inspire out of desire. Words of poetry that stir the heart and the songs that comes from the mouth of a lark; words of pain and words that sustain; words glorifying God in hymns of praise--written words of song placed with musical scores on sheets of paper.

In the Old Testament, harps were used to express the condition of the heart. **Psalm 49:4**. In **Psalm 137:2**, the people of Israel hung their harps up on poplars and wept because of their captivity in a foreign land. They refused to sing joyful songs to their captors. In the Book of Job, The lyre was used in mourning. **Job 30:31**. I like to think about the tumbrels and songs of God's deliverance.

# The Word of God is Superior to Man

Light up the World with His Word

God's wisdom is flawless and perfect; it is tranquil, gentle, truthful and fair; merciful and comforting; faithful and steadfast without hypocrisy. **James 3:17.**

When the heart and mind is clear and clean, so will the tongue be also. The solution to controlling our tongue is to seek divine wisdom and be slow to anger. God will help you to endure for I am a living testimony of how He has helped me to endure much suffering, reproach and hardship in my life. **James 1:19-21.**

*Gospel to be proclaimed before Christ's return –*

*Jesus instructs His twelve disciples –* **Matthew 10:6-7, 14**

Jesus said He is sending us out as sheep among wolves. **Matt. 10:16.** He also spoke about how we must be careful of men who would persecute us (we are witnessing the persecution of Christians today in the Middle East, Egypt, Africa, and other parts of the world). **Matt. 10:19-20.**

*Everyone is called, few of us are chosen.* Some give up because of reproach for the Christian life requires faith, humility, persecution, endurance, and discipline. The few are called, "a faithful remnant". Some make excuses like Moses. They tell God they are slow of speech **Exodus 4:10-11**. God's response was, "Who has made man's mouth?" If God created the mouth, we must use caution on how we use it. God does not look at age. In **Exodus 7:7** Moses was 80 years old and Aaron 83 when they spoke to Pharaoh.

# Prayer Our True Devotion

***Pray for a Godly Voice*** : Our true devotion is found in our prayer room thanking God that He has opened up a path to His throne. **Col. 4:2. *In Luke 18:1, Jesus encouraged us to pray.*** Be in readiness at all times and stay centered in constant prayer.

It is very important that we be very careful about what we say in prayer. We must never pray out of anger or jealousy. God told me many years ago that there was only one way to pray and that is, "Lord let Thy will be done." We should never pray our opinion or for something terrible to happen to someone. This leads us into the occult and spoken curses. To be safe, I pray the word of God and salvation for my enemies.

The word of God says if we have difficulty praying or don't know how to pray, the Holy Spirit gives us utterance. Because most people do not know how to pray for themselves or refuse to, God has raised up intercessors. I have the greatest respect and honor for intercessors because they seek the face of God with a pure heart on behalf of others. They humble themselves in proxy. The good news is that Jesus is our Intercessor as well.

**Hebrews 7:25**.

My prayer for you is found in **Romans 15:5-7**.

## *Prayers*

**Psalm 59:12** – Prayer for someone praying a curse over you or lying about you.

**Psalm 140:1-3** – Prayer for the Lord to preserve and rescue you from evil and violent men.

## *Prayers for the Tongue that Accuses*

The tongue of an accuser is doing the work of the devil. See **Revelation 12:9-10** and **Job 1:6-12**.

Prayers for your accusers: **Psm. 109:17-20** and **Psm. 109:26-29**.

## The Gift of the Holy Spirit

Speaking in tongues: Tongues is the Greek word

for known languages. We are encouraged to pray in our spiritual language. **Ephes. 6:18.**

**The Apostle Paul: I Corin. 14:5.**

**Pentecost: Acts 2:3-4** – (Baptism of Fire). Fire often indicated the presence of God. One example is the burning bush in **Exodus, Chapter 3:1-3. Exodus 13:21, 22.**

# The Promise and Command of God

In **Zephaniah 3:9, 13**.

God will purify our lips that we may call upon Him as we walk side by side with Him in life's journey. (v. 9)

We are commanded to not err or do wrong by telling lies and practicing deceit. (v. 13).

After reading these two scriptures, I realized how much we stumble and fall when our speech is not pleasing to God. Our service is hindered (verse 9) and we are full of fear (verse 13).

**Colossians 3:1-10**

# Pastor Regina's Comments

Expressions of old sayings like faux pas, social errors or misconduct with our tongue: "It's just a slip of the tongue" or "Putting one's foot in the mouth" is a very poor excuse for not giving enough thought to what we say before we say it. We touch people in different ways with our words. Sometimes our mouth doesn't grow with us and we tend to speak childish things out of our heart. When we grow with God's word, we obtain wisdom, knowledge, and understanding in using our words carefully during our journey on to maturity.

The power of life and death is in the tongue. **Prov. 18:21**.

With our mouths, we grumble and complain; we also call out many names and on occasion place blame. Our words are able to annunciate, communicate, and placate; we talk and talk as we walk. We express our passion in a romantic fashion and tell tales and fables around the table. We laugh out loud alone or in a crowd. We say what is on our mind and even pray if we are so inclined. But the best words to ever be heard with truth, purity, and charity; flows from heaven's throne and spoken by God alone now and throughout all eternity.

- **Pastor Regina**

Before I began writing, I use to write inside my head like I do on paper. I saw many words over the years. This is when I knew God was calling me to be a scribe in His kingdom. Word's come alive through books that opens up the heart of God----like His word. All paths lead to Christ Jesus. It is quite evident that in order to have the best communication possible, we must:

a) Pursue wisdom, the knowledge of God, and understanding in His word.

b) To avoid speaking wickedly and foolishly, our hearts and minds must be opened to teaching and correction.

c) Look at Jesus' example when we don't know

how or what to say.

Jesus has given us His authority and remedies in order to aid us in the process of having clean, loving, teachable, and understandable communication with others. Self-interests fails. When we improve our character, what comes out of our mouth becomes a more useful and desirable tool for God as well as man.

Those who are in agreement with God in speaking His truth is not ashamed of His gospel. Those who don't believe His truth are living a lie and the truth is not in them. Our spirit man is like a beautiful home that God created. The door represents our heart and mouth. It is up to us to keep it clean and in good repair. The Word of God helps us in this endeavor. God is our shelter from the storms that would destroy our homes and no one can clean a house better than He. So open up the windows of your hearing and let His light come inside.

If we just close our eyes, we can ride upon the cloud of God's word and live above the deceitful and lying tongues of the world. His Spirit searches the depths of His word and we will not only see His character and heart, smile at His promises, but also live and speak righteously and live as though His second coming is only a moment away.

I have a lot of words to say about words. I pray that this pouring out from God's word and mine will help you better communicate with God and man.

Choose your words carefully.

Divinely inspired,

Pastor Regina Brent

Extended Hands of Jesus

June 1, 2013 ; Revised February 2017

CPSIA information can be obtained
at www.ICGtesting.com
Printed in the USA
FFOW02n2239040917
39535FF